THE INSPIRATION OF THE SCRIPTURES

Loraine Boettner

GLH Publishing
LOUISVILLE, KY

Originally Published in 1937.
Copyright unrenewed, Public Domain

GLH Publishing Reprint, 2019

ISBN:
 Paperback 978-1-948648-77-6
 Epub 978-1-948648-78-3

*Sign up for updates from GLH Publishing
using the link below and receive a free ebook.*
http://eepurl.com/gj9V19

CONTENTS

1. The Nature of Scripture Inspiration 1
2. The Writers Claim Inspiration 12
3. The Nature of the Influence by Which Inspiration is Accomplished 24
4. The Alleged Errors in Scripture 32
5. The Trustworthiness of the Bible 47
6. The Plenary Inspiration of the Bible 58

1. The Nature of Scripture Inspiration

The answer that we are to give to the question, "What is Christianity?" depends quite largely on the view we take of Scripture. If we believe that the Bible is the very word of God and infallible, we will develop one conception of Christianity. If we believe that it is only a collection of human writings, perhaps considerably above the average in its spiritual and moral teachings but nevertheless containing many errors, we will develop a radically different conception of Christianity, if, indeed, what we then have can legitimately be called Christianity. Hence we can hardly over-estimate the importance of a correct doctrine concerning the inspiration of the Scriptures.

In all matters of controversy between Christians the Scriptures are accepted as the highest court of appeal. Historically they have been the common authority of Christendom. We believe that they contain one harmonious and sufficiently complete system of doctrine; that all of their parts are consistent with each other; and that it is our duty to trace out this consistency by a careful investigation of the meaning of particular passages. We have committed ourselves to this Book without reserve, and have based our creeds upon it. We have not made our appeal to an infallible Church, nor to a scholastic hierarchy, but to a trustworthy Bible, and have maintained that it is the word of God, that by His providential care it has been kept pure in all ages, and that it is the only inspired, infallible rule of faith and practice.

That the question of inspiration is of vital importance for the Christian Church is easily seen. If she has a definite and authoritative body of Scripture to which she can go, it is a comparatively easy task to formulate her doctrines. All she has to do is to search out the teachings of Scripture and embody them in her creed. But if the Scriptures are not authoritative, if they are to be corrected and edited and some parts are to be openly rejected, the Church has a much more difficult task, and there can be no end of conflicting opinions concerning either the purpose of the Church or the system of doctrine which she is to set forth. It is small wonder that determined controversy rages around this question today when Christianity is in a life and death struggle with unbelief.

It should be noted that the Church has not held all of her other doctrines with such tenacity, nor taught them with such clearness, as she has this doctrine of inspiration. For instance, there has been considerable difference of opinion between denominations as to what the Bible teaches concerning baptism, the Lord's Supper, predestination, inability of the sinner to do good works, election, atonement, grace, perseverance, etc.; but in the Scriptures we find this doctrine taught with such consistency and clearness that all branches of the Church, Protestant and Roman Catholic alike, have agreed with instinctive judgment that the Bible is trustworthy and that its pronouncements are final.

But while this has been the historic doctrine of Christendom, and while today it remains embedded in the official creeds of the churches, it is apparent on every side that unbelief has made serious inroads. Perhaps no event in recent Church History has been more amazing than the swing away from faith in the authority of the Scriptures. Even Protestants, who at the time of the Reformation took as their basic principle an authoritative Bible rather than an authoritative Church, have shown a great tendency to neglect the Bible. While numerous books and articles have been written on this subject in recent times, it must be admitted that most of these have been designed to explain away or to tone down the doctrines which the Church has held from the beginning.

The indifference which the Church has manifested toward sound Scripture doctrine in recent days is probably the chief cause of the uncertainty and of the internal dissension with which she is faced. Ignorance concerning the nature of the doctrine of inspiration, or want of clear views concerning it, can only result in confusion. Millions of Christians today are like men whose feet are on quicksand and whose heads are in a fog. They do not know what they believe concerning the inspiration and authority of the Bible.

Much of this uncertainty has arisen because of the searching critical investigation which has been carried on during the past century, and we often hear the claim made that the historic Church doctrine of the inspiration of the Scriptures must be given up. Hence the burning question today is, Can we still trust the Bible as a doctrinal guide, as an authoritative teacher of truth, or must we find a new basis for doctrine, and, consequently, develop a whole new system of theology?

The marvelous unity of the Bible can be explained on no other ground than that of divine authorship. It is confessedly one book, yet it is made up of sixty-six different books, composed by not less than forty writers, spread over a period of not less than sixteen hundred years. The writers moved in widely separated spheres of life. Some were kings and scholars with the best education that their day afforded; others were herdsmen and fishermen with no formal education. It is impossible that there should have been collusion between the writers. Yet there is but one type of doctrine and morality unfolded. The Messianic spirit and outlook pervades the Old Testament, beginning early in Genesis where we are told that the seed of the woman is to bruise the head of the serpent, and continuing through the ritual of the sacrificial system, the Psalms, the major and minor prophets until Malachi closes the Old Testament canon with the promise that "the Lord, whom ye seek, will suddenly come to his temple." And "Christ crucified" is the theme of the New Testament. The marvelous system of truth that is begun by Moses in the book of Genesis is brought to completion by John in the book of Revelation. In the development of no other book in the history of the world has there ever been anything that even remotely approaches this phenomenon that we find in the Bible.

That there is a wide and impassable gulf between the Bible and all other books is apparent to even the casual observer. "Holy, holy, holy" seems to be written on its every page. As we read, it speaks to us with authority and we instinctively feel ourselves under obligation to heed its warnings. It is certainly furnished with an influence which is possessed by no other book, and we are forced to ask the question, Whence comes it? And since it is so unique in the power which it exerts, so lofty in the moral and spiritual principles which it sets forth, and since it so repeatedly claims to be of divine origin, are we not justified in believing that claim to be true, that it is in fact the very word of God?

The terms "plenary inspiration" and "verbal inspiration" as used here are practically synonymous. By "plenary inspiration" we mean that a full and sufficient influence of the Holy Spirit extended to all parts of Scripture, rendering it an authoritative revelation from God, so that while the revelations come to us through the minds and wills of men they are nevertheless in the strictest sense the word of God. By "verbal inspiration" we mean that the Divine influence which surrounded the sacred writers extended not only to the general thoughts, but also to the very words they employed, so that the thoughts which God intended to reveal to us have been conveyed with infallible accuracy—that the writers were the organs of God in such a sense that what they said God said.

Inspiration Necessary to Secure Accuracy

That this inspiration should extend to the very words seems most natural since the purpose of inspiration is to secure an infallible record of truth. Thoughts and words are so inseparably connected that as a rule a change in words means a change in thought.

In human affairs, for instance, the man of business dictates his letters to his secretary in his own words in order that they may contain his exact meaning. He does not assume that his secretary will correctly express important, delicate, and complicated matters which might be given him in general terms. Much less would the Holy Spirit say to His penman, "Write to this effect." The Bible assumes to speak concerning a number of things which are absolutely beyond the reach of man's wisdom—the nature and attributes of God, the origin and purpose of man and of the world, man's fall into sin and his present helpless condition, the plan of redemption including our Lord's substitutionary life and death, the glories of heaven, and the torments of hell. More than a general supervision is necessary if the truth concerning these great and sublime subjects is to be given without error and without prejudice. Inerrancy requires that God shall choose His own words. All men who have tried to explain these deep things without supernatural revelation have done little more than show their own ignorance. They grope like the blind, they speculate and guess and generally leave us in greater uncertainty than before. In the nature of the case these things are beyond man's wisdom. We have only to look at the pagan systems or at the arrogant and speculative theories of our own philosophers to find what the limits of our spiritual wisdom would be apart from the Bible. Whether we turn to the philosophers among the Greeks, to the Mystics of the East or to the intellectuals among the Germans, the story is the same. In fact many of the world's supposedly advanced thinkers have even doubted the existence of God and the immortality of the soul. God alone is capable of speaking authoritatively on these subjects; and of all the world's books we find that the Bible alone gives us on the one hand an adequate account of the majesty of God, and on the other hand an adequate account of the sinful state of the human heart and a satisfactory remedy for that sin. It shows us that neither laws nor education can change the human heart, that nothing short of the redemptive power of Christ can make man what he ought to be.

A mere human report of divine things would naturally contain more or less error, both in regard to the words chosen to express the ideas and in the proportionate emphasis given the different parts of the revelation. Since particular thoughts are inseparably connected with particular words, the wording must be exact or the thoughts conveyed will be defective. If it be admitted, for instance, that the words, ransom, atonement, resurrection, immortality, etc., as used in Scripture have no definite authority or meaning behind them, then it follows that the doctrines based on them have no definite authority. In Scripture's own use of Scripture we are taught the stress which it lays upon the very words which it employs, the exact meaning depending upon the use of a particular word, as when our Lord says that "the Scripture cannot be broken" (John 10:35); or when He answered the Sadducees by referring them to the words spoken to Moses at the burning bush where the whole point of the argument depended on the tense of the verb, "I am the God of Abraham, and the God of Isaac, and the God of Jacob" (Mark 12:26); or when Paul stresses the fact that in the promise made to Abraham the word used is singular and not plural—"seed," "as of one," and not "seeds, as of many;" "And to thy seed, which is Christ" (Gal. 3:16). In each of these cases the argument turns on the use of one particular word, and in each case that word was decisive because it had divine authority behind it. Oftentimes the exact shade of meaning of the original words is of the utmost importance in deciding questions of doctrine and life.

A Definite System of Theology

For any serious study of Christian doctrines we must first of all have the assurance that the Bible is true. If it is a fully authoritative and trustworthy guide, then we will accept the doctrines which it sets forth. We may not be able to grasp the full meaning of all of these things, there may in fact be many difficulties in our minds concerning them; but that they are true we shall never doubt. We acknowledge our limitations, but we shall believe in so far as the truth has been revealed to us. The fortunes of distinctive Christianity are in a very real sense bound up with those of the Biblical doctrine of inspiration, for unless that stands we have nothing stable.

If we have a trustworthy Scripture as our guide, we shall have an evangelical, as distinguished from a naturalistic, humanistic or Unitarian system of theology; for we find the evangelical system clearly taught in the Bible. But if the Bible is not a trustworthy guide, we shall then have to seek a different basis for our theology, and the probability is that we shall have but little more than a philosophical system left. To undermine confidence in the Bible as an inspired Book is to undermine confidence in the whole Christian system. This truth is rather painfully impressed upon us when we attempt to read some of the recent religious books, even systematic theologies, in which the writers appeal not to Scripture but to the teachings of various philosophers to prove their points. If the Bible is not trustworthy we might as well save ourselves the labor of "revising" our creeds. We might as well throw them away and make a fresh start, for we shall then have to develop a whole new theology. To date we have accepted the distinctive doctrines of the Christian system because we found them taught in the Bible. But apart from the Bible we have no authoritative standard.

Unless the Bible can be quoted as an inspired book its authority and usefulness for public preaching, for comfort in sickness or death, and for instruction in every perplexity, have been seriously impoverished. Its "Thus saith the Lord" has then been reduced to a mere human supposition, and it can no longer be considered our perfect rule of faith and practice. If it cannot be quoted as an inspired book, its value as a weapon in controversy has been greatly weakened, perhaps entirely destroyed; for what good will it do to quote it to an opponent if he can reply that it is not authoritative? Today, as in every past age, the destructive critics, skeptics, and modernists of whatever kind center their attacks on the Bible. They must first be rid of its authority or their systems amount only to foolishness.

The inspiration for which we contend is, of course, that of the original Hebrew and Greek words as written by the prophets and apostles. We believe that if these are understood in their intended sense—plain statements of fact, figures of speech, idioms and poetry as such—the Bible is without an error from Genesis to Revelation. While it leaves much unsaid, we believe that all that it does say is true in the sense in which it is intended. We do not claim infallibility for the various versions and translations, such as the American Standard or King James versions, and much less do we claim infallibility for the rather free one man translations which have attained some vogue in recent years. Translations will naturally vary with each individual translator, and are to be considered accurate only in so far as they reproduce the original autographs. Furthermore, some of the Hebrew and Greek words have no full equivalent in the English language, and sometimes even the best scholars differ as to the exact meaning of certain words. And further still, we must acknowledge that we have none of the original autographs, but thatf our oldest manuscripts are copies of copies. Yet the best of the present day Hebrew and Greek scholars assert that in probably nine hundred and ninety-nine cases out of a thousand we have either positive knowledge or reasonable assurance as to what the original words were, so accurately have the copyists reproduced them and so faithfully have the translators done their work. Hence he who reads our English Bible as set forth in the American Standard or King James version has before him what is, for all practical purposes, the very word of God as it was originally given to the prophets and apostles. Certainly we have reason to thank God that the Bible has come down to us in such pure form.

This has been the historic Protestant position concerning the authority of Scripture. It was held by Luther and Calvin, and was written into the creeds of the post-Reformation period. The Lutheran doctrine of inspiration was set forth in the Form of Concord, which reads: "We believe, confess, and teach that the only rule and norm, according to which all dogmas and all doctors ought to be esteemed and judged, is no other whatever than the prophetic and apostolic writings of the Old and New Testament." The doctrine of the Reformed Church was stated in the Second Helvetic Confession as follows: "We believe and confess, that the canonical Scriptures of the holy prophets and apostles of each Testament are the true word of God, and that they possess sufficient authority from themselves alone and not from man. For God Himself spoke to the fathers, to the prophets, and to the apostles, and continues to speak to us through the Holy Scriptures." And in the Westminster Confession of Faith the Presbyterian Church declared that "It pleased the Lord, at sundry times and in divers manners, to reveal Himself and to declare His will unto His Church; and afterward...to commit the same wholly unto writing." "The authority of the Holy Scripture, for which it ought to be believed and obeyed, dependeth not upon the testimony of any man or church, but wholly upon God (who is truth itself) the author thereof; and therefore it is to be received because it is the word of God." And further that both the Old and New Testament have been "immediately inspired by God and by His singular care and providence kept pure in all ages." In more recent times it has been reasserted by Hodge, Warfield and Kuyper. That these men have been the lights and ornaments of the highest type of Christianity will be admitted by practically all Protestants. They have held that the Bible does not merely *contain* the word of God, as a pile of chaff contains some wheat, but that the Bible in all its parts *is* the word of God.

2. THE WRITERS CLAIM INSPIRATION

Our primary reasons for holding that the Bible is the inspired Word of God are that the writers themselves claim this inspiration, and that the contents of their messages bear out that claim. The uniformity with which the prophets insisted that the messages which they spoke were not theirs but the Lord's—that their messages were the pure and unmixed Word of God, spoken out by them just as they had received them—is a striking phenomenon of Scripture. "Thus saith the Lord" was the prophet's constant reminder to the people that the words which he spoke were not his own, but God's. Paul and the other apostles claimed to speak not in the words which man's wisdom taught, but in words which the Spirit taught (1 Cor. 2:13). Not only the substance of their teaching, but also its form of expression, was asserted to be of Divine origin.

Although the claim that they spoke with Divine authority is characteristic of the writers throughout the entire Bible, they never once base that authority on their own wisdom or dignity. They speak as the Lord's messengers or witnesses, and their words are to be obeyed only because His authority is behind them. Those who heard them heard God, and those who refused to hear them refused to hear God (Ezek. 2:5; Matt. 10:40; John 13:20).

2. THE WRITERS CLAIM INSPIRATION

And since the writers so repeatedly claimed inspiration, it is evident that they were either inspired or that they acted with fanatical presumption. We are shut up to the conclusion that the Bible is the Word of God, or that it is a lie. But how could a lie have exerted the uniquely beneficial and morally uplifting influence that the Bible has exerted everywhere it has gone? To ask such a question is to answer it.

Let us also notice that the contemporaries of the New Testament writers, as well as the early church fathers—men who were in the best position to judge whether or not such claims were true—accepted these claims without question. They acknowledged that a great gulf existed between those writings and their own. As to the dying Sir Walter Scott there was but one "Book," so to these early church fathers there was but one authoritative Divine word. They based doctrines and precepts on it. The Gospels and Epistles contain an abundance of internal evidence showing that they were expected to be received and that they were received with reverence and humility. And as we follow the course of history down through the centuries the evidence becomes all the more abundant. Even the heretics bear witness to this fact, anxious as they are to be rid of such authority. Furthermore, the writings themselves contain no contradictions or inconsistencies which would destroy their claims. With perfect harmony they present the same plan of salvation and the same exalted moral principles. If, then, in the first place, sober and honest writers claim that their words were inspired by God; and if, in the second place, these claims not only went unchallenged but were humbly accepted by their contemporaries; and if, in the third place, the writings contain no contradictory evidence, then certainly we have a phenomenon which must be accounted for.

Objection is sometimes made to the New Testament books on the ground that they are not the writings of Jesus but only of His followers, and that they were not written until some time after His death. But it is hardly to be expected that Jesus would have given a full account of the way of salvation during His earthly ministry, for that could not have been understood until after His death and resurrection. He could, indeed, have set it forth by way of prophecy even in the days of His flesh, and in fact He announced to His disciples the general nature of the plan. But even His most intimate disciples appear to have been unable to understand the nature of His work until their minds were enlightened by the Holy Spirit on the day of Pentecost. All things considered, the most natural method was that which He chose—the fulfillment of the events, and then their explanation through inspired writers. That, also, was in accordance with the Lord's procedure throughout Old Testament times.

Scripture Teaching Concerning Inspiration

The Biblical doctrine of the true purpose and function of the prophets and their manner of delivering the message is clearly set forth in the Lord's words to Moses: "I will raise them up a prophet from among their brethren, like unto thee; *and I will put my words in his mouth, and he shall speak unto them all that I shall command him*" (Deut. 18:18). Jehovah would speak not so much to the prophets as through them. They were to speak precisely the words given them, but no others. "I have put my words in thy mouth," the Lord said to Jeremiah in appointing him a prophet to the nations (Jer. 1:9). Identically the same words were spoken to Isaiah (51:16; 59:21), and the formula, "Thus saith Jehovah," is repeated some eighty times in the book of Isaiah alone. Even the false prophet Balaam could speak only that which Jehovah gave him to speak—"And the angel of Jehovah said unto Balaam, Go with the men; but only the word that I shall speak unto thee, that thou shalt speak" (Nu. 22:35; 23:5, 12, 16). In many Old Testament passages it is nothing other than a process of "dictation" which is described, although we are not told what the method was by which this dictation was accomplished. In others we are simply given to understand that Jehovah spoke through chosen men as His organs, supervising them in such a manner that their spoken or written words were His words and were a distinctly superhuman product. The uniform teaching of the Old Testament is that the prophets spoke when, and only when, the word of Jehovah came unto them: Hosea 1:1; Amos 1:3; Micah 1:1; Malachi 1:1, etc.

The characteristic Hebrew word for prophet is *nabhi*, "spokesman," not merely spokesman in general, but by way of eminence, that is, God's spokesman. In no case does the prophet presume to speak on his own authority. That he is a prophet in the first place is not of his own choosing, but in response to a call from God, oftentimes a call which was obeyed only with reluctance: and he speaks or forbears to speak as the Lord gives him utterance.

And in strong contrast with this high calling of the true prophets we should notice the stern warnings and denunciations against those who presume to speak without having received a Divine call. "But the prophet that shall speak a word presumptuously in my name, which I have not commanded him to speak, or that shall speak in the name of other gods, that same prophet shall die" (Deut. 18:20); "Woe unto the foolish prophets, that follow their own spirit, and have seen nothing" (Ezek. 13:3). It is a serious thing for mere men, with unwashen hands, to presume to speak for the Most High. Yet how common it is for the destructive critics of our day to deny this or that statement in the Bible, or to tell us that we need a shorter Bible, or perhaps even a new Bible composed of modern writings! And the error committed by men in adding to God's word, as the Roman Catholics do with their "Apocrypha" and church traditions, the Christian Scientists with their "Science and Health With Key to the Scriptures," and the Mormons with their "Book of Mormon," is fully as bad as to take from it.

Testimony of Jesus to the Old Testament

That Jesus considered the Old Testament fully inspired is abundantly clear. He quoted it as such, and based His teachings upon it. One of His clearest statements is found in John 10:35, where, in controversy with the Jews, His defense takes the form of an appeal to Scripture, and after quoting a statement He adds the significant words, "And the Scripture cannot be broken." The reason that it was worth while for Him, or that it is worth while for us, to appeal to Scripture, is that it "cannot be broken." And the word here translated "broken" is the common one for breaking the law, or the Sabbath, meaning to annul, or deny, or withstand its authority. In this statement Jesus declares that it is impassible to annul, or withstand, or deny the Scripture. For Him and for the Jews alike, an appeal to Scripture was an appeal to an authority whose determination was final even to its minute details.

That Jesus considered all Scripture as the very word of God is shown in such a passage as Matt. 19:4. When some of the Pharisees questioned Him on the subject of divorce His reply was: "Have ye not read, that he who made them from the beginning made them male and female, and said, 'For this cause shall a man leave his father and mother, and shall cleave to his wife; and the two shall become one flesh.... What therefore God hath joined together, let not man put asunder." Here He explicitly declares that God is the author of the words of Gen. 2:24: "*He who made them...said*," "A man shall leave his father and mother, and shall cleave to his wife." And yet as we read these words in the Old Testament there is nothing to tell us that they are the words of God. They are presented only as the words of Scripture itself or of Moses, and can be assigned to God as their Author only on the basis that all Scripture is His word. Mark 10:5–9 and 1 Cor. 6:16 present the same teaching. Wherever Christ and the Apostles quote Scripture, they think of it as the living voice of God and therefore divinely authoritative. They have not the slightest hesitation in assigning to God the words of the human authors, or in assigning to the human authors the most express words of God (Matt. 15:7; Mark 7:6, 10; Rom. 10:5, 19, 20).

In His stinging rebuke to the Sadducees, "Ye do err, not knowing the Scriptures" (Matt. 22:29), the very thing which He points out is that their error comes, not because they have followed the Scriptures, but precisely because they have not followed them. He who founds his doctrine and practice on Scripture does not err. So common was its use, and so unquestionable was its authority, that in the fiercest conflict He needed no other weapon than the final "It is written"! (Matt. 4:4, 7, 10;

Luke 4:4, 8; 24:26). His last words before His Ascension contained a rebuke to the disciples because they had not understood that all things which were written in the entire Scriptures "must needs be fulfilled" (Luke 24:44). If it was written that the Christ should suffer these things, then all doubt concerning Him was rendered absurd. The disciples were to rest securely on that word as on a sure foundation. Hence we receive the Old Testament on the authority of Christ. He hands it to us and tells us that it is the Word of God, that the prophets spoke by the Spirit, and that the Scriptures cannot be broken. By His numerous quotations He has welded it to the New Testament so that they now form one unified Bible. The two Testaments have but one voice. They must stand or fall together.

New Testament Manner of Quoting the Old Testament

If Jesus held that the entire Old Testament was infallible, the idea is no less clearly set forth by the Apostles. The familiar way in which they quote any part of the Scriptures as the word of God, regardless of whether the original words are assigned to Him or not, shows that He was considered as speaking all through the Old Testament. In Heb. 3:7 the words of the psalmist are quoted as the direct words of the Holy Spirit, "Wherefore, even as the Holy Spirit saith, Today if ye shall hear his voice, Harden not your hearts, as in the provocation" (Ps. 95:7). In Acts 13:35 the words of David (Ps. 16:10) are said to have been the words of God, "He (God) saith in another psalm, Thou wilt not give thy Holy One to see corruption." In Romans 15:11 the words of the psalmist are ascribed to God, "And again (He saith), Praise the Lord, all ye Gentiles; And let all the peoples praise Him" (Ps. 117:1). In Acts 4:24, 25 the Apostles ascribe to God the words spoken by David in the second psalm, "God...who by the Holy Spirit, by the mouth of our father David thy servant, didst say, Why do the Gentiles rage, And the peoples imagine vain things?" In Hebrews 1:7, 8 the same teaching is found concerning two other psalms. In Romans 15:10 the words of Moses are ascribed to God, "And again He saith, Rejoice, ye Gentiles, with His people" (Deut. 32:43).

These quotations show clearly that in the minds of Christ and the Apostles there was an absolute identification between the text of the Old Testament and the voice of the living God. And it is, of course, not to be inferred that the inspiration of the New Testament is in any way inferior to that of the Old. In fact the tendency has been to assign a lower position to the Old Testament. When the Old Testament is shown to be inspired there is usually no question about the New.

CLAIMS OF THE NEW TESTAMENT WRITERS FOR THEIR OWN WRITINGS

When we examine the claims which the New Testament writers make for their own works we find that they claim full inspiration for them and place them on the same level with the Scriptures of the Old Testament. All schools of present-day Biblical criticism acknowledge that these claims were repeatedly made, even though they deny that they are true. We find, for instance, that when the Apostles began their ministry they received from Christ Himself a promise of supernatural guidance: "But when they deliver you up, be not anxious how or what ye shall speak: for it shall be given you in that hour what ye shall speak. For it is not ye that speak, but the Spirit of your Father that speaketh in you" (Matt. 10:19, 20; Mark 13:11; Luke 12:11, 12). This same promise was repeated at the close of His ministry (Luke 21:12–15). Perhaps the most important promise is found in the Gospel of John: "When He, the Spirit of truth, is come, He shall guide you into all the truth" (16:13). The Apostles later claimed this guidance. They have not the least shadow of doubt as to the exact truth of their words, whether on historical or doctrinal matters,—a rather striking phenomenon, since accurate and truth-loving historians commonly express less, and not greater, assurance when they descend to details. So authoritative does Paul claim his gospel to be that he pronounces wrong and accursed any one who teaches differently, even though it be an angel from heaven. "… But though we, or an angel from heaven, should preach unto you any gospel other than that which we preached unto you, let him be anathema…" (Gal. 1:6–9). Their commands are from the Lord, and are given with binding authority, "…the things which I write unto you, that they are the commandment of the Lord" (1 Cor. 14:37,; 2 Thess. 3:6, 12). In writing to the Corinthians Paul distinguishes between the commands which Christ gave, and the commands which he gives, but places his own alongside those of Christ's as of equal authority (1 Cor. 7:10, 12, 40). He asserts that what they preached was in truth "the word of God" (1 Thess. 2:13). Such things were to be immediately and unquestionably received. We should also notice his easy way of combining the book of Deuteronomy and the Gospel of Luke under the common head of "Scripture," as if that were a most natural thing to do (1 Tim. 5:18): "For the Scripture saith, Thou shalt not muzzle the ox when he treadeth out the corn. And, the laborer is worthy of his hire" (Deut. 25:4;

Luke 10:7). This same practice was common among the early church fathers.

In 2 Tim. 3:16 (translating the Greek in its most natural sense) Paul tells us that "All scripture is given by inspiration of God, and is profitable for doctrine, for reproof, for correction, for instruction in righteousness." This marginal translation, which has behind it the, authority of Archbishop Trench, Bishop Wordsworth, and others of the Revised Version Committee, as well as the authority of that prince of exegetes and theologians, Dr. Benjamin B. Warfield, is much to be preferred to the rendering of the Revised Version, which reads, "Every scripture inspired of God is profitable," etc. This latter translation has been repudiated by numerous scholars as a calamitous and hopelessly condemned blunder, and even by some of the critics as false criticism. As Dr. Warfield has pointed out, the very term in the Greek, *theopneustos*, means not that a product of human origin is breathed into by God, but that a Divine product is breathed out by God. It means "God breathed," "produced by the creative breath of the Almighty," "God-given." There is no other term in the Greek language which would have asserted more emphatically the Divine origin of the product.

In the writings of Peter we find the same high estimate of New Testament Scripture. He declares, for instance, that "No prophecy ever came by the will of man: but men spake from God, being moved (or literally, *borne, carried along*) by the Holy Spirit" (2 Peter 1:21). He declares that the Apostles "preached the Gospel… by the Holy Spirit sent forth from heaven" (1 Peter 1:12). He places Paul's writings on the same high plane with "the other scriptures" — "Our beloved brother Paul also, according to the wisdom given to him, wrote unto you; in all his epistles...as also the other scriptures" (2 Peter 3:15, 16). More dignity and reverence and authority than that could not be ascribed to any writing.

Luke declares that on the day of Pentecost the disciples spoke "as the Spirit gave them utterance" (Acts 2:4). And John, the beloved disciple, even pronounces a curse on any one who dares to take from or add to his writing (Rev. 22:18, 19). Such claims as these, if based only on human authority, would exhibit only the most astounding impudence.

It is, of course, impossible to explain away the innumerable texts which teach plenary inspiration, and the idea that they might be explained away is based on the odd notion that this doctrine is taught only in isolated texts here and there. It is true that some texts teach it with exceptional clearness, and those are the ones which skeptics would most like to be rid of. But these passages are simply the climax of a progressive and pervasive testimony to the divine origin and infallibility of these writings, a testimony equally strong in the two Testaments. "The effort to explain away the Bible's witness to its plenary inspiration," says Dr. Warfield, "reminds one of a man standing safely in his laboratory and elaborately explaining—possibly with the aid of diagrams and mathematical *formulae*—how every stone in an avalanche has a defined pathway and may easily be dodged by one with some presence of mind. We may fancy such an elaborate trifler's triumph as he would analyze the avalanche into its constituent stones, and demonstrate of stone after stone that its pathway is definite, limited, and may easily be avoided. But avalanches, unfortunately, do not come upon us stone by stone, one at a time, courteously leaving us opportunity to withdraw from the pathway of each in turn: but all at once, in a roaring mass of destruction. Just so we may explain away a text or two which teach plenary inspiration, to our own closest satisfaction, dealing with them each without reference to its relation to the others: but these texts of ours, again, unfortunately do not come upon us in this artificial isolation; neither are they few in number. There are scores, hundreds, of them; and they come bursting upon us in one solid mass. Explain them away? We should have to explain away the whole New Testament. What a pity it is that we cannot see and feel the avalanche of texts beneath which we lie hopelessly buried, as clearly as we may see and feel the avalanche of stones! Let us, however, but open our eyes to the variety and pervasiveness of the New Testament witness to its high estimate of Scripture, and we shall no longer wonder that modern scholarship finds itself compelled to allow that the Christian Church has read her records correctly, and that the church-doctrine of inspiration is simply a transcript of the biblical doctrine; nor shall we any longer wonder that the church, receiving these Scriptures as her authoritative teacher of doctrine, adopted in the very beginning of her life the doctrine of plenary inspiration, and has held it with a tenacity that knows no wavering, until the present hour."

3. The Nature of the Influence by Which Inspiration is Accomplished

The evangelical Christian churches have never held what has been stigmatized the "mechanical" theory of inspiration, despite the charges often made to the contrary. Instead of reducing the writers of Scripture to the level of machines or typewriters we have insisted that, while they wrote or spoke as they were moved by the Holy Spirit, they nevertheless remained thinking, willing, self-conscious beings whose peculiar styles and mannerisms are clearly traceable in their writings. If their native tongue was Hebrew, they wrote Hebrew; if it was Greek, they wrote Greek; if they were educated, they wrote as men of culture; if uneducated, they wrote as such men would write. We do not separate the divine and human elements, but insist that the two are united in perfect harmony so that every word of Scripture is at one and the same time the word of God and also the word of man. The writers themselves make it plain that in this process the divine influence is primary and the human secondary, so that they are not so much the originators but rather the receivers and announcers of these messages. Hence what they wrote or spoke was not to be looked upon as merely their own product, but as the pure Word of God, and for that reason it was to be received and implicitly obeyed.

The fact that we can so easily trace the peculiar style or manner of expression through the writings of Paul or John or Moses shows that the Scriptures were given in a way which made allowance for human personalities. If it were otherwise the Scriptures would then be reduced to a dead level of monotony, and we would indeed have a mechanical theory of inspiration in which the writers were little more than automatons. It lies in the very idea of inspiration that God would use the agents which He employs according to their individual natures. One type of man would be chosen to write history, another type to write poetry, and still another type to set forth doctrines, although these functions might overlap in some writers. And back of that we are to remember that throughout the entire life of the prophet God's providential control had been preparing him with the particular talents, education and experience which would be needed for the message which he was to give. This providential preparation of the prophets, which gave them the proper spiritual, intellectual and physical background, must, indeed have had its beginning in their remote ancestors. The result was that the right men were brought to the right places at the right times, and wrote the particular books or gave the particular messages which were designed for them. When God wanted to give His people a history of their early beginnings, He prepared a Moses to write it. When He wanted to give them the lofty and worshipful poetry of the psalms, He prepared a David with poetic imagination. And since Christianity in its very nature would demand logical statement, He prepared a Paul, giving him a logical mind and the appropriate religious background which would enable him to set it forth in that manner. In this natural way God so prepared the various writers of Scripture that with the appropriate assistance of His directing and illuminating Spirit they freely and spontaneously wrote what He wished as He wished and when He wished. Thus the prophet was fitted to the message, and the message was suited to the prophet. Thus also the distinctive literary style of each writer was preserved, and each writer did a work which no one else was equipped to do.

On some occasions inspiration amounted to little if anything more than a process of dictation. God spoke and man recorded the words: Gen. 22:15–18; Ex. 20:1–17; Is. 43:1–28, etc. On other occasions the writers functioned as thinkers and composers with all of their native energy coming into play as they deliberated, recollected and poured out their hearts to God, the Holy Spirit exercising only a general supervision which led them to write what was needful and to keep their writings free from error, e.g., Luke 1:1–4; Rom. 1:1–32; Eph. 1:1–23, etc. In narrating simple historical facts and in copying lists of names or numbers from reliable sources this superintendence was at a minimum. Perhaps in some instances they were not even conscious of the Spirit's directing influence as they wrote.

In the main, however, we can say that the words of the prophets express not merely something which has been thought out, inferred, hoped or feared by them, but something conveyed to them,—sometimes an unwelcome message forced upon them by the revealing Spirit. They naturally shrank from giving messages which foretold destruction for the people or for the nation. Yet they were not at liberty to say either more or less than what had been given to them, for he who is entrusted with a message from the King is not at liberty to omit or change any part of it but must give it out just as he has received it. Isaiah, for instance, immediately after his glorious vision and official appointment, was sent with an unwelcome message to his countrymen, and was even told beforehand that the people would not hear, that the effect of his preaching would be further rebellion and further hardening of their hearts. Yet he was not able to change the message, but could only inquire, "Lord, how long?" (Is. 6:9–13). Ezekiel likewise was sent to a rebellious people and was told that they would not hear (3:4–11) But whether they would hear or whether they would forbear, they were to know that a prophet of the Lord had been among them (Ezek. 2:5). Much as the prophet might like to speak otherwise, he could only give the message which had been given to him. If the people failed to heed the warning the responsibility rested on themselves (Ezek. 33:1–11). The objectivity of the message is further shown in that sometimes the prophets themselves did not understand the revelations which were given through them (Daniel 12:8, 9; Rev. 5:1–4).

Nor is the work of the Holy Spirit in inspiration to be considered any more mysterious than His work in the spheres of grace and providence. The first exercise of saving faith in the regenerated soul, for instance, is at one and the same time a work induced by the Holy Spirit and a freely chosen act of the person. And throughout the Bible the laws of nature, the course of history, and the varying fortunes of individuals are ever attributed to God's providential control. "Jehovah hath His way in the whirlwind and in the storm, and the clouds are the dust of His feet," Nahum 1:3. "He maketh His sun to rise on the evil and the good, and sendeth rain on the just and the unjust," Matt. 5:45. "The Most High ruleth in the kingdom of men, and giveth it to whomsoever

He will, and setteth up over it the lowest of men," Dan. 4:17. "It is God who worketh in you both to will and to work, for His good pleasure," Phil. 2:13. "The king's heart is in the hand of Jehovah as the watercourses: He turneth it whithersoever He will," Prov. 21:1.

Inspiration must have been somewhat like the touch of the driver on the reins of the racing steeds. The preservation of the individual styles and mannerisms indicates as much. Under this providential control the prophets were so governed that while their humanity was not superseded their words to the people were God's words and have been accepted as such by the Church in all ages.

That the writers of Scripture often used other documents or sources in the composition of their books is apparent to even the casual reader. For instance, the thirty-seventh chapter of Isaiah and the nineteenth chapter of 2 Kings are exactly alike. Hence Isaiah and the writer of 2 Kings must have had access to the same source materials. Many of the accounts in the different Gospels are told in almost identical language. If it be definitely proven, for instance, that the Pentateuch consists of different parts which in turn are based on older documents, our doctrine of inspiration can accept that view. In dealing with historical or legal data especially the writers of Scripture may have used sources as naturally as do present-day writers, with this difference: that the Holy Spirit supervised their work in such a way that they selected out only the material which God wanted given to the people, and set forth that material in such a way that it was free from error. We are not so much concerned with the method by which they wrote as we are about the value and authority of their final product. The more naturally and the less mechanically this writing took place, the better.

It is not to be expected that we should give a full explanation as to how the divine and human agents co-operated in the production of Scripture. Suffice it to say that in most cases it was something much more intimate than what is commonly known as "dictation." The trouble with us is that oftentimes we seek full explanations for those things which in their deeper aspects should only be adored as mysteries, such as the Trinity, the atonement, the relationship between the sovereignty of God and the freedom of man, and the inspiration of the Scriptures. The modernist with his naturalistic basis easily solves these problems by ignoring the Divine, but is unaware how superficial he is. Evangelicals have truly grappled with these problems. They have acknowledged both the Divine and human elements and have brought about a partial solution while confessing that the human mind cannot fully comprehend the deep things of God.

It is, of course, not to be assumed that inspiration rendered the prophets omniscient. Their inspiration extended only to the contents of the particular messages which were given through them. In matters of science, philosophy or history which were outside their immediate purpose they stood on the same level with their contemporaries. They were preserved from error when speaking the Lord's message, but inspiration in itself no more made them astronomers or chemists than it made them agriculturists. Many of them may have believed with their contemporaries that the sun moved around the earth, but nowhere in their writings do they teach that it does. Paul could not err in his teachings, although he could not remember how many people he had baptized at Corinth (1 Cor. 1:16). We have already observed that Daniel and John did not fully understand all the revelations given through them. Isaac unwittingly pronounced the prophetic blessing on Jacob instead of his favorite son Esau, and when he later discovered that he had been deceived he was utterly unable to change it. When Moses recorded the promise that Abraham was to be the father of many nations, he little realized that in the later era all of the Gentile Christians were to be included in that promise and that eventually it would embrace the whole world (Gal. 3:29; Eph. 2:13, 14; Rom. 4:13; Acts 13:17).

Nor does the doctrine of inspiration imply that the writers were free from error in their personal conduct. Moses wrote voluminously concerning the early history of Israel and is commonly considered the greatest of the Old Testament prophets; yet at the waters of Meribah he took to himself the glory which belonged only to Jehovah, and for that offense he was not permitted to enter the promised land (Nu. 20:7–13). Balaam spoke certain great truths, and Saul was among the prophets. Peter likewise was infallible as a spokesman of the Lord, and yet on at least one occasion he fell into serious error in his personal conduct and it was necessary for Paul to resist him to the face, for he stood condemned (Gal. 2:11–14).

Furthermore, we find that inspiration was flexible enough to allow for some personal matters, as when Paul asked Timothy to come to him shortly and to bring his coat and certain books which he had left at Troas (2 Tim. 4:13). It includes personal advice in regard to Timothy's health, (1 Tim. 5:23), and personal concern for the treatment accorded to the returned slave Onesimus (Philemon 1:10–16).

Hence we see that the Christian doctrine of inspiration is not the mechanical lifeless process which unfriendly critics have often represented it to be. Rather it calls the whole personality of the prophet into action, giving full play to his own literary style and mannerisms, taking into consideration the preparation given the prophet in order that he might deliver a particular kind of message, and allowing for the use of other documents or sources of information as these were needed. If these facts were kept more clearly in mind the doctrine of inspiration would not be so summarily set aside nor so unreasonably attacked by otherwise cautious and reverent scholars.

4. The Alleged Errors in Scripture

One of the most distressing things in present-day churches is that whereas in the religious debates of earlier days they used to argue about what the Bible said, never for a moment doubting that what it said was true, groups within the various churches are now arguing as to whether or not the Bible is trustworthy. A short time ago the writer heard a sermon by a professor from a well-known theological institution in which he declared that the Bible contained historical, moral and literary errors. This is a serious charge and if it could be proved it certainly would destroy the Christian doctrine of inspiration.

That the Bible contains some statements which we in our present state of knowledge are not able to explain fully, is readily admitted. Our knowledge of the Hebrew and Greek languages is by no means perfect. There are a number of words or idioms, for instance, which occur only once or only a few times in Scripture, and it sometimes happens that even the best scholars are not in full agreement as to their exact meaning.

It gives us no little satisfaction, however, to know that as scholarship and archaeological discovery have advanced the great majority of the supposed "Biblical errors" which were so confidently paraded by skeptics and atheists a few decades ago have been cleared up.

4. The Alleged Errors in Scripture

Today scarcely a shred of the old list remains. It gives us even greater satisfaction to know that despite all of the merciless attacks which through the ages have been made on the Bible, and despite all of the fierce light of criticism which so long has been beating upon its open pages, *not so much as one single error has been definitely proved to exist anywhere in the Bible*. Without exception up to the present time where the conflict has been joined and the verdict rendered the skeptic has been proved wrong and the Bible right. Those supposed discrepancies remain today as only too readily forgotten warnings against those who in their eagerness to do violence to the Scripture doctrine of inerrancy throw historical and literary caution to the winds.

It is to be noted further that the alleged errors have been for the most part trivial. In no cases have important doctrines or important historical events been in question. When fuller light is turned on them most of them, like ghosts, melt away from sight. Few if any of them are anything more than mistakes on the part of copyists or translators; and certainly no one has a right to say there are errors in the Bible unless he can show beyond reasonable doubt that they were in the original manuscripts.

The few difficulties which still remain are so trivial that no one should be seriously troubled by them. There is every reason for believing that with additional knowledge they too will be cleared up. It is little exaggeration to say that on the whole they bear about the same relation to the Bible that a few grains of sandstone detected here and there in the marble of the Parthenon bear to that building. In view of past experience it is important to keep in mind that there is a strong presumption against any of them being real errors, a presumption which can be measured only by the whole weight of evidence which can be brought forward to prove that the Bible is a fully trustworthy guide in moral and spiritual matters.

When we remember that the Bible was in process of being written over a period of about fifteen hundred years, that some forty authors living in different ages with different points of view in life and with diverse literary talents had a part in its production, that the religious and political history of the country was hopelessly complicated, and that confessedly accurate Roman historians have sometimes fallen into error in narrating contemporary events, the marvel is, not that there are a few things recorded in the Bible which are difficult to understand, but that the number is so few.

Even though it be admitted that the Bible contains some few statements which we in our present state of knowledge are not able to harmonize, that should afford no rational ground for denying the general doctrine of Scripture infallibility. We have the word of Christ Himself that "the Scripture cannot be broken" (John 10:35); and more than that we should not ask. In the material universe we see evidences of design so manifold, and diverse, and wonderful, that the mind is driven to the conclusion that it has an intelligent Author. And yet here and there we find monstrosities. The fact that in our present state of knowledge we are not able to explain fully why snakes and mosquitoes and malaria germs were created does not prevent us from believing that the world had an intelligent and benevolent Creator. Neither should the Christian give up his faith in a fully inspired Bible just because he is unable to harmonize every detail with all of the remainder.

Perhaps no other science in recent times has done so much to confirm the Bible as has archaeology. The patient work of explorers and excavators in Egypt, Babylonia, Assyria and Palestine, with their picks and shovels, has opened volumes of ancient history for us, giving us graphic accounts of the languages, literature, institutions and religions of peoples who had long since been forgotten except as they were incidentally mentioned in the Bible. Here we have the records chiseled in stone, burnt into the clay brick tablets, recorded in one way or another on the monuments, tombs, buildings, papyrus and pottery. Without exceptions these discoveries confirm the truthfulness of the Bible, and time after time the theories and guesses of the destructive critics have been proved wrong. In fact the enemies of the Bible have met no more relentless foe than the science of archaeology. The evidence presented from this source is so impartial, unimpeachable and conclusive that it compels acceptance by friend and foe alike.

Examples of Alleged Errors

Space forbids us giving a detailed list of the "errors" which have been pointed out in Scripture, yet our discussion would be incomplete if we did not give a few examples. At first sight there seems to be a contradiction between Acts 9:7 and Acts 22:9 concerning the conversion of Saul. In the former it is said that the men who traveled with Saul heard the voice which spoke to him, while in the latter it is said they did not hear the voice. The difficulty is solved, however, by the fact that the Greek word translated "voice" may also mean "sound" and is so translated in the marginal reference given with Acts 9:7. We conclude that the men who were traveling with Saul heard the sound, but did not understand the words.

It has been only a few years since the destructive critics had nothing but scorn for any one who accepted Luke's statements that the island of Cyprus was ruled by a "pro-consul" (Acts 13:7), and that Lysanias was a contemporary tetrarch with the Herodian rulers (Luke 3:1). Yet how quickly the scorn was forgotten when archaeological discovery vindicated the Biblical statements.

Whether in the healing of the centurion's servant the centurion himself went to Jesus and asked that his servant be healed, as Matthew leads us to believe (8:5), or whether he sent unto Him elders of the Jews as Luke says (7:3), is all the same so far as the point of the story is concerned. In our everyday language we ascribe to the person the thing which his agents or servants do at his command.

The accusation which Pilate wrote on the cross is given with slight variations by the different Gospel writers: It appears, however, that the explanation for this is to be found mainly in the fact that the accusation was written in three languages, in Latin, Greek and Hebrew, that there were variations in the originals, and that at least one of the writers may have given a free translation, there being no substantial difference for instance between Mark's statement, "The King of the Jews," and Luke's statement, "This is the King of the Jews."

Whether on the resurrection morning the stone was rolled away from the tomb by human hands, as we might infer from the accounts given by Mark, Luke and John (although they are careful not to say that it was by human hands, but only that the stone was rolled away), or whether an earthquake was used to serve the purpose as Matthew more specifically tells us (28:2), makes no difference in regard to the essential point of the story that Christ arose and came forth from the tomb on that morning. Matthew has given the account in greater detail at this point, telling us that the Lord used the forces of nature to accomplish His purpose, while the other writers have simply recorded the important religious truth that the tomb was opened. It often happens that the sacred writers, like secular writers, describe events from different points of view or with different points of emphasis. In cases of this kind there is no more contradiction between the narratives than there is, for instance, between four photographs of the same house, one of which is taken from the west, another from the north, another from the east, and another from the south, although they may present quite different views.

Matt. 27:5 says that Judas brought his money back to the priests, then went out and hanged himself, while Acts 1:18 says that he obtained a field with his money. But weaving together the two fuller accounts it appears that what really happened was that when the priests rejected the money Judas threw it down in the temple and then went out and hanged himself. But after his treachery and suicide such disgrace attached to him that no friends or relatives came to care for the body and that it had to be buried at public expense. The priests remembered that his money had been brought back, that it could not be put into the treasury since it was blood money; and now that his body needed burial they very appropriately decided to use the money to buy a burial ground, perhaps the very field in which he had committed suicide. Hence he is said to have obtained a field with the reward of his iniquity,—not that he personally bought it, but that it was purchased with his money and he was buried in it.

Many critics claim that the reference to Jeremiah in Matt. 27:9 is an error, and that the reference should have been to Zechariah (11:12, 13). This, however, seems to be a case of "Subsequent Mention," such as Acts 20:35 and Jude 14. Matthew says that Jeremiah "spoke" these words, and certainly no one can prove otherwise. Apparently Jeremiah spoke them, Zechariah wrote them down, and Matthew, under the guidance of the Holy Spirit, quoted them and assigned them to Jeremiah. Perhaps Matthew had other books which assigned them to Jeremiah but which have since been lost. The fact that Matthew's quotation is not quite the same as that found in Zechariah may also indicate that he possessed other books.

It is sometimes said that in Gen. 36:31 the reference to the "king" (or kings) who ruled over the children of Israel proves that the book of Genesis was not written by Moses but by some later person. We are to remember however, that Moses was a prophet, that long before this the promise had been given to Abraham that kings would arise (Gen. 17:6; 35:11), that Moses himself predicted the rise of kings in Israel (Deut. 17:14–20), and that in Gen. 36:31 he simply says that kings were reigning in Edom before any had yet arisen in Israel.

In regard to Ex. 9:19 it is sometimes asked how the Egyptians could have had any cattle left to be killed by the hail, which was the seventh plague, when Ex. 9:6 declares that all of them had been killed by the murrain, which was the fifth plague. This is explained, however, by the fact that the fifth plague did not kill the cattle which belonged to the Israelites, and that during the time which had elapsed between the fifth and seventh plagues the Egyptians doubtless had taken possession of many of those.

The fact that the Ten Commandments as given in Exodus 20:3–17 and Deut. 5:7–21 shows some variation in wording, or that in a number of instances where the New Testament writers have quoted from the Old Testament they have not given the exact words but only the general meaning, is no argument against verbal inspiration unless it can be proved that they intended to quote *verbatim*. A writer or speaker is entirely within his rights if he chooses to repeat his thoughts in a somewhat different form, and this is what the Holy Spirit has done. Human language at its best is too imperfect to express the fullness of the Divine Mind, and we should not limit the Holy Spirit to a sterotyped form of speech. The New Testament writers are often more concerned to give the basic truth, setting it forth with variety and richness, than they are to follow a stereotyped form. This consideration sets aside a large number of the contradictions which some critics profess to find in the Bible. Furthermore, if we find a passage which is capable of two interpretations, one of which harmonizes with the rest of Scripture while the other does not, we are duty bound to accept the former. Whether the statement in question be in Scripture, in historical records, or in legal documents, the accepted principle of interpretation is that the meaning which assumes the document to be self-consistent and reasonable is to be preferred to the one which makes it inconsistent and unreasonable. To act on any other basis is to act with prejudice and to assume error rather than to prove it. The critics of the Bible, however, have often been only too glad to neglect this rule.

Many of the so-called "moral difficulties" of the Old Testament arise only because people fail to take into consideration the progressive nature of revelation. Much more, of course, is expected of us who live in the Christian era and who have the full light of the New Testament than was expected of those who lived in the former ages. Here too there is "first the blade, then the ear, then the full corn in the ear." Sometimes misunderstanding arises because of failure to distinguish between what the Scriptures record and what they sanction.

Probably the most serious problems arise in regard to matters such as the destruction of the Canaanites, the imprecatory Psalms, the substitutionary doctrine of the atonement, and the doctrine of eternal punishments. We may not be able to solve all the difficulties connected with these, but the objection that they are morally wrong proceeds on the assumption that there can be no such thing as retributive justice. We must remember, however, that while God is good and rewards righteousness, He is also just and most certainly punishes sin, and that the punishment of sin is as obligatory on Him and reflects His glory as truly as does the rewarding of righteousness. This is taught in the New Testament as clearly as in the Old, and it is at the basis of the doctrine that the punishment for our sins could not simply be cancelled but had to be laid on Christ if we were to be saved. Furthermore, the Old Testament teaches that not only certain individuals but sometimes whole towns and tribes were so degraded that they were a curse to society and unfit to live. Even the religion of some tribes was desperately corrupt, that of Baal and Ashtaroth, for instance, being accompanied by lascivious rites, the sacrifice of newborn children in the fire by their parents, and the kissing of the images of these heathen gods.

The Old Testament attitude toward polygamy, divorce, slavery, intoxicants, and kindred themes, is often ridiculed by present-day critics, but if seen in its proper setting is itself an argument for the divine origin of the Bible. In regard to almost all such questions we find that the design of the Bible is to set forth basic principles which shall be applicable to all peoples and races and in all ages rather than to give specific laws which while suited to one type of people under certain social conditions might not be equally suited to others. The making of specific laws governing social and civil affairs and suited to local conditions is left largely to later legislative bodies. Consequently the laws of the Bible are not as specific as many people would like them to be. In regard to the use of intoxicants, for instance, we certainly are told that "Wine is a mocker, strong drink a brawler; And whosoever erreth thereby is not wise," Prov. 20:1; that no drunkard shall inherit the kingdom of God 1 Cor. 6:10; that we are not to spend our money for that which is not bread, Is. 55:2; and many other similar statements. On the basis of these we should be able to frame suitable legislation dealing with the liquor traffic. The wisdom which the Bible showed in dealing with those evils in a primitive age—giving laws and principles which regulated them, and in regulating destroyed them—is strong evidence in itself that the law is of superhuman origin.

The Bible and Science

The Bible, of course, was not written from the scientific point of view, and the person who attempts to deal with it as if it were a textbook on science will be badly disappointed. Written long before the rise of modern science, it was intended primarily not for scientists and intellectuals but for the common people. Its language is that of the common people, and its subject matter is primarily religious and spiritual. Had it been written in the language of modern science or philosophy it would have been unintelligible to the people of earlier ages, and in fact would also be unintelligible to multitudes in our own day. Moreover, while we certainly have no desire to disparage the scientific accomplishments of our day but wish rather to accept them and use them to the full, we must point out that textbooks on science have to be rewritten at least once every generation and that so rapidly is scientific research progressing in our day that most books on scientific subjects are obsolete within ten years. But in the Bible we have a Book which has had no revision for multiplied centuries and which appeals to the heart and intelligence of people today as strongly as it has ever done in the past. Those who go to the Bible for spiritual and intellectual inspiration find it as fresh and inspiring as if it had been written but yesterday.

One of the most marvelous things about the Bible is that although it was written in a day of ancient ignorance and superstition it does not contain the popular errors and fallacies of that day. Moses as the Crown Prince of Egypt attended the best of their schools and "was instructed in all the wisdom of the Egyptians"—most of which is considered pure nonsense today—but he did not write that in his books. The weird and fantastic theories held by the Egyptians concerning the origin of the world and of man were passed over completely; and in the first chapter of Genesis in majestic language which has never been surpassed to this day he gives an account of God's creation of the world and of man, no statement of which is disproved by modern science. Other prophets who were in contact with the Chaldean and Babylonian science were equally guided so that while personally they may have believed many things which were erroneous they wrote only what was in harmony with the truth.

Some of the prophets may have believed, for instance, that the world was flat. But nowhere in their writings do they teach us that it is flat. When they speak of the sun rising and setting, or of the four corners of the earth, or of the ends of the earth, we are not to take those expressions literally. We use the same expressions today, but we do not mean to affirm that the sun goes around the earth, or that the earth is flat or rectangular. In our everyday speech we often describe things as they appear, rather than as they are known to be. And while skeptics as a class are ever ready to affirm that the Bible teaches that the world is flat, hardly one can be found who is honest enough to quote the one particular verse in which the Bible *does* make a statement about the shape of the earth. In describing the greatness and majesty of God Isaiah says that "He sitteth above the circle of the earth,"—the Hebrew word translated "circle" literally means "roundness" (40:22). Nor are the skeptics any more anxious to quote Job's statement when in contrast with the popular ideas of his day he wrote, "He stretcheth out the north over the empty space, And hangeth the earth upon nothing" (26:7).

In the year 1861 the French Academy of Science published a list of fifty-one so-called scientific facts, each of which, it was alleged, disproved some statement in the Bible. Today the Bible remains as it was then, but not one of those fifty-one so-called facts is held by men of science.

Distinction should always be made between the speculations in the realm of science and its clearly proven facts. The speculations of science are like the shifting currents of the sea, while the Scriptures have breasted them like the rock of Gibralter for two thousand years. The Bible has not been shown to contradict so much as one proven fact of science; on the contrary the account which it presents of the origin and order of the world, as contrasted with that found in other ancient books, corresponds with the findings of modern science to a degree that is perfectly marvelous. The conflict which some people suppose to exist between the Bible and science simply does not exist.

Perhaps the primary reason there has been so much confusion regarding the relationship between religion and science is the failure on the part of so many people to discriminate between facts and opinions. True science deals only with established facts; opinions may be as varied as the people who express them. Organic evolution, for instance, as it is usually set forth rules out the supernatural and contradicts the Bible. But it must be remembered that organic evolution is not science, but only a theory, an hypothesis. Not one of the five arguments usually advanced to support it is sound, and many distinguished scientists do not believe in the theory of organic evolution but in fiat creation as taught in the Bible. A minister who has not studied science has no right to invade the domain of science and speak freely about it. Neither does a scientist who has had no experience in the motivating and regenerating power of the Holy Spirit have any right to invade the field of religion and speak freely about that. There have been numerous instances in recent years where outstanding scientists, with no special religious training, have presumed to write or speak their minds quite freely on religious subjects. But their opinions concerning religion are worth no more than are those of any other person—for the simple reason that they are assuming to speak concerning things outside of their legitimate field. The mere fact that a man is an authority within his own field does not entitle him to speak authoritatively on subjects outside of that field. True religion and true science never contradict each other but individual ministers and individual scientists will differ endlessly. Science has indeed done many marvelous things. But its domain is strictly limited to the material side of life. It has no authority to speak concerning spiritual things. Where it has been made a substitute for religion it has invariably turned out to be a false Messiah.

The relationship between the Bible and science has been quite clearly set forth by Dr. Samuel G. Craig in the following paragraph:

"It is one thing to say that the Scriptures contain statements out of harmony with the teachings of modern science and philosophy and a distinctly different thing to say that they contain proved errors. Strictly speaking there is no modern science and philosophy but only modern scientists and philosophers—who differ endlessly among themselves. It is only on the assumption that the discordant voices of present-day scientists and philosophers are to be identified with the voice of Science and Philosophy that we are warranted in saying that the Bible contains errors because its teachings do not always agree with the teachings of these scientists and philosophers. Does any one really believe that Science and Philosophy have yet reached, even approximately, their final form? May it not rather be contended that they are so far removed from their ultimate form that if the teachings of the Bible were in complete harmony with present-day science and philosophy it is altogether certain that they would be out of harmony with the science and philosophy of the future? If, for example, the anti-supernaturalism of the dominant science and philosophy of today is to be characteristic of science and philosophy in their final forms, then, unquestionably the Bible contains many errors. Who, however, is competent to assert that this will be the case? But unless it is certain that the science and philosophy of the future will be essentially one with the dominant science and philosophy of today, we go beyond the evidence when we say that the Bible contains proved errors on the ground that its teachings contradict the teachings of present-day scientists and philosophers."[1]

---

1 *Christianity Rightly So Called*, p. 217)

5. The Trustworthiness of the Bible

After a survey of the alleged errors and discrepancies, including not only the typical ones just mentioned, but also many others, we assert, without fear of successful contradiction, that no one of these is real. As Christians we call this book the "Holy Bible." But if it were only a relatively good book, setting forth many valuable moral and spiritual truths, but also containing many things which are not true, we would then have no right to apply to it the adjective "holy." It would then be on a level with other books, and would differ from them not in kind but only in degree.

But how different is our attitude toward it when we approach it as the very word of God, an inspired, infallible rule of faith and practice! How readily we accept its statements of fact and bow before its enunciations of duty! How instinctively we tremble before its threatenings, and rest upon its promises! As we proclaim the word of life from the pulpit, or in the classroom; as we attempt to give comfort at some bed of sickness, or in a bereaved home; or as we see our fellow-men struggling against temptation or weighed down with care, and would give them encouragement and hope for this world and the next, how thankful we then are for a fully trustworthy Bible! In such cases we want to know that we have not merely something that is probable or plausible, but something that is sure.

What might be called The Law of Ancient Documents, generally accepted by scholars in the study of either religious or secular books, is that "Documents apparently ancient, not bearing upon their face the marks of forgery, and found in proper custody, are presumed to be genuine until sufficient evidence is brought to the contrary." Now we submit that judged by this principle the books of both the Old and the New Testament are what they profess to be and that they should be accepted at face value. We are confident that when the critics are through, when the battle is over and the smoke has all been cleared away, the books of the Bible, if they could but speak, would say to us what Paul said to the Philippian jailor: "Do thyself no harm: for *we are all here*."

It seems rather difficult at first to understand why so many persons have busied themselves to point out errors in the Bible. But when we look a little more closely we find that this is a book which judges men and points out the sin of the heart. Unconverted man does not like this, and would much prefer to read a newspaper or a sensational novel. An account of a trial in one of our criminal courts interests him a great deal more than does a chapter in the New Testament. And since he does not like to have the truth told about himself and the world in which he lives, he tries to pick flaws in the blessed Book. The reason that he cannot leave it alone is that it does not leave him alone. Infidels in every age and from every class have labored hard to find out some errors which would convict the Scriptures of falsehood. They find no pleasure in pointing out errors in Virgil, or Cicero, or Shakespeare; but the Bible they cannot endure. And, sad to say, the determined enemies of the Word are to be found not only in the ranks of the vulgar and coarse, but also among the refined and cultured. Time and again those who have nothing else in common will, nevertheless, agree in their determined opposition to the Bible.

Testimony of Outstanding Scholars

In modern times there are, of course, many scholars who for various reasons attempt to discredit the written word. They usually begin by attacking the Old Testament and then carry their attack over into the New Testament. We are glad to say, however, that there are many other scholars of at least equal learning and skill who declare that the Bible is fully reliable. The late Dr. Benjamin B. Warfield, who for thirty-three years was Professor of Systematic Theology in Princeton Theological Seminary, was, we believe, the greatest systematic theologian and Greek scholar that America has produced. After having examined the evidence on which the destructive critics base their conclusions he had no hesitation whatever in pronouncing that evidence utterly worthless, and in declaring that the Bible from Genesis to Revelation is what it claims to be, the very word of God. His recently published book, *Revelation and Inspiration*, is undoubtedly the best book on the subject.[2] *The Sunday School Times* had abundant reason for pronouncing it "the most learned, exhaustive and convincing defense of the verbal inspiration of the Bible which has appeared in modern times," and in adding that "Dr. Warfield's acquaintance with sources, and his pointing out errors of opponents in quoting sources,

---

[2] Reprinted 1948, under the title, *The Inspiration and Authority of the Bible*.

seems fairly uncanny. If this book were widely read it would serve as a decisive check upon the many vagaries of 'inspiration' with which the believer is now confronted."

In regard to the Old Testament we feel reasonably safe in asserting that no greater authority has arisen in modern times than Dr. Robert D. Wilson. Possessed of a working knowledge of forty-five languages and dialects, and probably knowing more about the Old Testament than did any other man, his conclusion was set forth in the following words: "For forty-five years continuously I have devoted myself to the one great study of the Old Testament in all its languages, in all its archaeology, in all its translations, and, so far as possible, everything bearing upon its text and history...The evidence in our possession has convinced me that 'at sundry times and in divers manners God spake unto our fathers through the prophets,' and that the Old Testament in Hebrew, 'being immediately inspired by God,' has 'by His singular care and providence been kept pure in all ages'." Dr. Wilson's book, *A Scientific Investigation of the Old Testament*, in which his evidence and conclusions are set forth in simple and convincing language, and a more recent book, *The Five Books of Moses*, by Dr. Oswald T. Allis, who probably is the outstanding Old Testament scholar of the present day, should be read by every person who would be well informed concerning these matters.

The world still awaits a theory which will render an adequate account of the origin and authority of the Bible on any other hypothesis than that it came from God. One after another of the theories which have been advanced have fallen of their own weight or have been disproved by other destructive schemes. Up to date no hypothesis except that of divine origin has been able to maintain itself for as much as half a century. This in itself is a confession that the origin of the book cannot be accounted for by any other means than that given by the prophets themselves. Nor have we reason to believe that any more successful theory will arise in the future. Hence the only rational course for us to follow is to accept the Bible for what it professes to be until we can account for it by some other means.

It is interesting to note that down through the ages the orthodox Christian faith has been developed and set forth through the reverent and patient and anxious care of the Origens and Augustines, the Luthers and Calvins, the Hodges and Warfields, who believed the Bible to be fully inspired, and not by the Pelagians and Socinians, the Wellhausens and Fosdicks, with their superficial doubts as to whether Moses or Paul or even Christ and the apostles meant very much by what they said. May there never be occasion for people to say of us what was said of those of old time, that we received the word of God as it was ordained by angels, and kept it not.

Grounds for Our Belief That the Bible Is Infallible

When we assert that the Bible is completely trustworthy whether as regards its factual, doctrinal or ethical representations, we do not mean that we have personally examined each and every statement of the Bible with such care that we feel justified in asserting that they are all true, nor do we imply that we are possessed of omniscience. We reach that conclusion by first noting the claims which the Bible makes for its own inspiration and trustworthiness, and then testing those claims by the facts which are given us through Biblical criticism and exegesis. In view of the many evidences which substantiate this claim, such as the lofty moral and spiritual level which is maintained throughout the book, the promised guidance of the Holy Spirit, the many prophecies which were made in certain ages and fulfilled in detail in later ages, the inherent unity of the book, the simple and unprejudiced manner in which the accounts are given, etc., and in the absence of any proved errors, we conclude that the Bible is what it claims to be, a fully inspired book. This seems to be the only logical and proper way to approach the problem. If we reject this method, then, in order to arrive at a conclusion, we must make a comprehensive examination of every part of Scripture, taking it verse by verse, statement by statement, and prove its truth or falsity. But if we attempt this method it is not long until we come up against things hard to understand, statements concerning which we do not have adequate information, and prophecies which are as yet unfulfilled. We soon find ourselves, like certain persons of old, wresting the Scriptures to our own intellectual destruction.

The position of Conservative scholarship concerning this question has been presented clearly and convincingly by Dr. Samuel G. Craig. After stating that "the Bible bears witness to its own complete trustworthiness," he adds: "If that were not the case, the most we could possibly say would be that the Bible is without proved errors. That is obvious when it is remembered that even the latest parts of the Bible were written nearly two thousand years ago, that the Bible as a whole deals with periods of history with which at best we are imperfectly informed, that it relates the beliefs and experiences of many individuals of whom we know but little, that it contains representations alleged to have been supernaturally revealed, including many predictions not yet fulfilled—not to mention other matters. No one, not even the greatest scholar, has even a fraction of that knowledge that would be required to warrant him in affirming, on the basis of his knowledge alone, that the Bible is free from error. The case, however, is quite different, it seems to us, if testimony of their own complete trustworthiness is itself a part of the phenomena of Scripture. Then the way is open to assert their complete trustworthiness without first proving a universal negative. We would not be understood as implying that the mere fact that the Bible claims infallibility relieves us of the responsibility of examining its passages to ascertain whether its contents accord with the claim. However, if the Bible makes this claim and if even the most careful examination of its contents discloses nothing that contradicts it, it is at least possible that the claim is a valid claim. If on examining the Bible we find that all its statements that we are able to verify are trustworthy we will be more and more disposed to believe that the statements that are incapable of verification are also trustworthy. Our warrant, in brief, for asserting the inerrancy of the Bible is (1) *the absence of proved errors* and (2) *the witness which the Bible bears to its own complete trustworthiness*. (Italics ours.) Our confidence in the trustworthiness of the writers of the Bible is such that we feel fully warranted in accepting their statements as true even when we have no means of verifying them." And again, "We are dependent on the Scriptures for our knowledge of all the distinctive facts and doctrines of Christianity. If we cannot trust them when they tell us about themselves, how can we trust them when they tell us about the deity of Christ, redemption in His blood, justification by faith, regeneration by the Holy Spirit, the resurrection of the body and life everlasting?"[3]

Furthermore, the importance of the testimony of the Scriptures to their own trustworthiness is not fully realized unless we keep in mind the fact that the trustworthiness of Christ is equally involved. In the words, "The Scripture cannot be broken," and "Till heaven and earth pass away, one jot or one tittle shall in no wise pass away from the law until all things be accomplished," He ascribed absolute authority to the Scriptures of the Old Testament as an organic whole and made them the rule of life. At these points there is no question about the purity of the Greek text. Repeatedly He quoted the Scripture as final. Hence the authority of Scripture and the authority of Christ are inseparably connected. There are some, of course, who bow before Him and rejoice in Him as their Lord and Master while at the same time they ascribe not only historical but moral faults to the Scriptures. But such an inconsistent attitude cannot long be maintained. It seems absurd that we should be at the same time His worshippers and His critics. Only ignorance or lack of thought makes it possible for any person to suppose that he can remain orthodox in his conception of Jesus while accepting many of the views set forth by the destructive critics. When we reach the place where we say, "Jesus taught so and so, but the real truth of the matter is thus and thus," we simply cannot any longer worship Him as Lord and Master. Hence the question, "What think ye of Christ? whose son is He?" is closely parallel to the question, What think ye of the Bible? whose book is it? Investigation convinces us that the Bible, like the Christ which it sets

---

3 *Christianity Rightly So Called*, p. 226.

forth, is truly human and truly divine. As He was true man, in all points tempted like as we are, yet without sin, because also divine, so the Bible is a truly human book, written by men like ourselves, yet without error, because also divine.

When we say that inspiration extends to all parts of the Bible we do not mean to say that all parts are equally important. It is readily admitted that Genesis, or Matthew, or Revelation, for instance, is of much greater importance than Second Chronicles, or Haggai, or Jude. As Paul tells us, "One star differeth from another star in glory," —yet God made them all. In the human body some organs are of vastly greater value than others, the eyes or heart, for instance, as compared with the fingers, or toes, or hair. In fact, we can even do without certain organs if necessary, although a whole body is much more normal, healthy and desirable. And so it is with the Bible; not all parts are equally valuable, but all parts are equally true.

And further, we do not mean to say that had there been no inspiration there could have been no Christianity. We readily admit that had the writers of Scripture been shut up to their unaided faculties, as ordinary historians and teachers, they might, nevertheless, have given us fairly true and accurate accounts of the messages they received and of the events which took place, and that Christianity might have continued, although no doubt in a greatly impoverished form. Even if the Bible as a book had become completely lost the essential truths concerning the way of salvation might have been handed down to us with some degree of purity. But to what uncertainties, and doubts, and errors constantly begetting worse errors, we would then have been exposed! That we would then have had only a very weak and diluted form of Christianity will hardly be denied. To see what our fate would have been we need only look at such groups as the Roman Catholic or Greek Catholic Church, or at the Nestorian or Coptic churches, yes, and at present day Modernism with its untrustworthy Bible and its endless confusion. In the first two of these churches the people have been denied access to the Scriptures; in the other two they have had the Scriptures but with a large mixture of error. Without the Bible, then, we might still have had a form of Christianity; but, O, how much poorer we should have been! What a privilege it is to have in our hands a book every line of which was given by inspiration of God!—to have a divinely given history of the past, the present, and the future! Who can estimate aright such a privilege as this? As a matter of practical experience the strongest single factor making for the persistence of true Christianity and of righteousness in general down through the ages has been a fully trustworthy Bible in the hands of the common people.

We believe that the Bible as we now have it is complete, and that no new books are ever to be added. We believe this because the Bible gives us a sufficiently clear account of the relationship which exists between God and men, and of God's plan of redemption as it has been worked out by Christ and as it is now being applied to His people by the Holy Spirit. This is the view set forth in the Westminster Confession: "The whole counsel of God, concerning all things necessary for His own glory, man's salvation, faith, and life, is either expressly set down in Scripture, or by good and necessary consequence may be deduced from Scripture: unto which nothing at any time is to be added, whether by new revelations of the Spirit or traditions of men."

5. The Trustworthiness of the Bible

It should be kept in mind that the Protestant doctrine concerning the inspiration and authority of Scripture differs considerably from that held by the Roman Catholic Church. The Council of Trent, which met in the Italian city by that name and which concluded its sessions in the year 1653, set standards that the Roman Catholic Church has held quite consistently ever since. It affirmed the divine inspiration and authority of Scripture, but with some reservations. It declared that the Vulgate, which was St. Jerome's Latin translation of the Bible, and which was completed in the year 405, was the "authentic" text of Scripture, and that "no one is to dare or to presume to reject it under any pretext whatever." Furthermore, and more important, it introduced a fundamentally different estimate of the place of authority in religion, and of religion itself, when it put alongside of the Scriptures as of equal authority certain traditions of the church, consisting mainly of decrees issued by the popes and by church councils, and declared that the church alone was to be acknowledged as "the judge of the true sense and interpretation of the Holy Scriptures." This, of course, puts the final authority for the interpretation of Scripture in the hands of fallible and sinful men, and opens wide the floodgate to all kinds of error.

6. The Plenary Inspiration of the Bible

Inconsistent Position of the Modernists

We have already said that so-called Modernists or Liberals have no consistent stopping place. They must either go clear over to rationalism and barren negation, or they must turn back again to an authoritative Scripture. The history of Protestant Liberalism shows us very clearly that it has had extreme difficulty in maintaining itself even on the platform of theism, to say nothing of that of Christianity. Its tendency has been constantly downgrade, a progressive repudiation of all the fundamentals of the Christian faith. The Modernist, if he proceeds logically in the direction which his premises carry him, denies, first, the inspiration of the Scriptures, then the miracles, then the deity of Christ, then the atonement, then the resurrection, and finally, if he goes to the end of his road, he ends up in absolute skepticism. New England Unitarianism affords an example of this very thing. Strange as the words may sound in our ears, it is not uncommon in some places in America today to hear the "atheistic shade" of modern theology spoken of. There is, unfortunately for some, a happy consistency in the processes of reason which drives the various philosophical and religious systems to their logical conclusions.

6. The Plenary Inspiration of the Bible

Practically all evangelical churches require those who are ordained to the ministry to take a public vow that they accept the Bible as the Word of God. In the Presbyterian Church, U.S.A., for instance, every minister and elder at his ordination solemnly vows before God and men that he "believes the Scriptures of the Old and New Testaments to be the *Word of God*, the only *infallible* rule of faith and practice." (Italics ours.)[4] Since this confession is thoroughly evangelical it means that none but evangelicals can honestly and intelligently accept this ordination. A Modernist has not the slightest right to be a minister or elder in an evangelical church, and any Modernist who does become such lacks good morality as well as good theology. To declare one thing while believing the contrary is hardly consistent with the character of an honest man. And yet while our ordination vows are so thoroughly evangelical, how many there are even among the ministers of our churches who either deny or pass lightly over this basic Christian truth, the infallibility of the Scriptures!

Sometimes those who hold a low view of inspiration attempt to evade the issue by merely saying that the Bible *contains* the word of God. This loose formula, however, means practically nothing. A river in India, "rolling down its golden sands," certainly *contains* gold. But just what the relative proportion is between the sand and the gold may be very hard to determine. If the Bible only *contains* the Word of God, as even the Modernist is willing to admit, then certainly it may lack a great deal of being infallible, and we are then left to the mercies of "Higher Criticism," or to our own individual opinions, as to just which elements are the words of God and which are only the words of man.

---

4 Form of Government, XIII:IV; XV:XII.

As Dr. Clarence E. Macartney has recently said, "Those who have departed from faith in an infallible Bible have made desperate, but utterly vain efforts, to secure a suitable substitute and other standing ground. But as time goes by, the pathetic hopelessness of this effort is more and more manifest. Such catchwords as 'progressive revelation,' 'personal experience,' 'devotion to the truth,' etc., are one by one being cast into the discard. Modernism and Liberalism, by the confession of their own adherents, are terribly bankrupt, nothing but 'cracked cisterns,' into which men lower in vain their vessels for the water of life. There is no plausible substitute for an inspired Bible. No one can preach with the power and influence of him who draws a sword bathed in heaven, and who goes into the pulpit with a 'Thus saith the Lord' back of him...When man faces the overwhelming facts of sin, passion, pain, sorrow, death, and the beyond-death, the glib and easy phrases of current Modernism and flippant Liberalism are found to be nothing but a broken reed. Therefore, he who preaches historic Christianity and takes his stand upon a divine revelation has, amid the storms and confusions and darkness of our present day, an incomparable position.... There are not wanting signs today that men will return to the Holy Scripture, to drink again of the Water of Life and strengthen their souls with the Bread of Life, and that a prodigal Church, sick of the husks of the far country, will return to its Father's house."

Those who reject the Church doctrine of inspiration in favor of some lowered form have never been able to agree among themselves as to which parts of the Bible are inspired and which are not, or to what extent any part is inspired. If this high doctrine of verbal inspiration is rejected, there is no consistent stopping place short of saying that the Scripture writers were inspired only as was Shakespeare, or Milton, or Tennyson; and in fact some of the critics have consistently followed out their premises and have reached that conclusion. We submit, however, that if the other miracles recorded in Scripture be accepted there is no logical reason for rejecting the miracle of inspiration, for inspiration is simply a miracle in the realm of speaking or writing. Most of the objections which are brought against the doctrine today can be traced more or less clearly to the assumption that the supernatural is impossible.

Assurance That the Bible Is the Word of God

The question naturally arises, How are we to *know* that the Bible is the Word of God? We reply: *By the witness of the Holy Spirit within our hearts as we read*. As the Christian reads the Bible he instinctively feels that God is speaking to him. The Holy Spirit bears witness with his spirit that these things are so, the primary and decisive grounds for his conviction being not external but internal. To the spiritually illuminated the word is self-authenticating. He does, indeed, find much additional assurance to be had in noting the many incomparable excellencies of the writings, such as the lofty spiritual and moral truths set forth, the unity of all the parts, the majesty of the style, the uniformly uplifting influence of the Bible wherever it has gone, its appeal at one and the same time to the learned philosopher and to the poor black man of the jungle, its statement of truth in such simple language that even a child can grasp its meaning while even the most learned man cannot exhaust its depths, the minute fulfillment of prophecies centuries after they were spoken, etc. These are, indeed, proofs which should compel acceptance, and they can be effectively used to stop the mouths of objectors; but in the final analysis they are of subordinate value only. Apart from the inner illumination of the Holy Spirit they will not convince the unbeliever, no matter how logically and skillfully they may be presented.

The attempt to prove the divine origin of the Bible from these external criteria is similar to that of proving the existence of God from the external world. We may cite the ontological, the teleological, the cosmological, and the moral arguments, and the evidence seems convincing enough to the believer. Yet none of these arguments are demonstrative and coercive, and they usually leave the skeptics unconvinced. When we consent to stake the authority of Scripture on external arguments we are consenting to fight the battle on the field of our opponents' choosing, and we then simply have to make the best of a vulnerable position. These arguments in themselves are of such a nature as to invite doubt in the unregenerate mind, and they can never permanently settle the question. When we consent to fight the battle on these grounds we are making a concession to Rationalism, a system which assumes that the human reason is capable of sitting in judgment upon and evaluating all human experiences, and which denies the necessity of any divine revelation whatsoever.

In our deepest selves we are either regenerate or unregenerate. Paul tells us that "the natural (unregenerate) man receiveth not the things of the Spirit of God: for they are foolishness unto him; and he cannot know them, because they are spiritually judged" (1 Cor. 2:14); and again he says that the gospel of Christ crucified is "unto Jews a stumbling block, and unto Gentiles foolishness"; but unto them that are called, both Jews and Greeks, it is "the power of God, and the wisdom of God" unto salvation (1 Cor. 1:23, 24). Consequently the unregenerate man assumes an antagonistic attitude, and will not be convinced by any amount of external testimony. Ultimately every person has to make a choice between the *vox Dei* and the *vox mundi*, the voice of God and the voice of the world; and the question as to which of these he acknowledges to be the more authoritative is determined by whether the soul is regenerate or unregenerate. It is as impossible for the unaided human reason to understand the deep things of the Spirit as it is for the ordinary psychologist to give an adequate explanation of the process of conversion. Every attempt to convince the unregenerate soul of the divine origin of the Bible by means of scholarly and historical proof can only result in failure, and must be given up as completely as when Jesus forebore to convince the members of the Sanhedrin that he was not guilty of blasphemy when they had made up their minds to the contrary. This was the principle for which the Protestant Church stood at the time of the Reformation. While the Roman Catholics acknowledged the Church as the source of authority, and the Humanists acknowledged the human reason, the Protestant principle, as it was given typical expression for instance in the Westminster Confession, was the voice of God speaking in the soul. "The authority of the Holy Scripture, for which it ought to be believed and obeyed, dependeth not upon the testimony of any man or church, but wholly upon God (who is truth itself), the author thereof; and therefore it is to be received, because it is the Word of God... Our full persuasion and assurance of the infallible truth, and divine authority thereof, is from the inward work of the Holy Spirit, bearing witness by and with the word in our hearts" (I:IV, V). We would doubtless make better progress in our present day discussions if we kept that principle in mind.

In the final analysis, then, the Christian's faith does not depend upon external proofs, but upon an inner experience. He lives by the Scripture and enjoys its light. He has an inner conscious assurance—call it mysticism or whatever you will—that he is a child of God, and that the Scriptures are the word of God. The external proofs help to clarify and strengthen his faith, but his absolute and inescapable proof that the Christian system in general is the true system is found in the witness of the Holy Spirit in his heart as he reads and in his experience as a Christian. Although he may not be possessed of scholarly and scientific evidence which would enable him to meet the destructive critics on their own ground, he repels all their doubts in the same manner as did the blind man who was healed by the Saviour, and who replied to every argument of the Pharisees with the immovable conviction of certainty: "Whether he is a sinner, I know not: one thing I know, that, whereas I was blind, now I see." He no more asks permission of the critic to believe than he asks permission of the scientist to breathe, but finds both most natural and spontaneous. He does, indeed, find that truly scientific and scholarly study gives clearer direction to the word, and that it enables him to systematize and understand it better. But his authority for belief is from the heart rather than from the reasoning processes of the head.

This does not mean that we deprecate scholarship. Nowhere has the principle of sound scholarship and scientific investigation existed in a healthier state than in the loyal sons of the Evangelical churches. In fact, we are persuaded that except for the service which scholarship has rendered, the Christian faith would have been well-nigh helpless against the attacks of unbelief. We desire a solid historical foundation for our faith, and our investigation shows that we have such. We acknowledge that the external proofs, when presented to unbelievers in a reasonable way, point the way to God and often prepare the heart for the gracious work of the Holy Spirit. But we simply wish to point out that these proofs which are relied upon so heavily by some are ineffective unless supplemented by the work of the Holy Spirit in the heart.

Our opponents will probably complain that this method of procedure gives a strong dogmatic cast to the discussion. They forget, however, that they proceed in exactly the same way: they too proceed from premises which are as axiomatic, even though they profess to be particularly subject to reason. Their axiom is that the human reason is competent to judge all things, even the deep things of God. While we acknowledge that theirs is also a dogmatic procedure, we do not complain about it, since they *cannot* do otherwise—the mind which has not been enlightened by the Spirit is not able to discern the things of the Spirit. As Thornwall has fittingly said, "the reality of evidence is one thing, the power to perceive it, is quite another. It is no objection to the brilliancy of the sun if it fails to illuminate the blind." We each have our fixed method of procedure. All we can ask is that these principles be put to a practical test, and that we be given opportunity to see which best squares with the experiences of life and reality.

Conclusion

In conclusion, then, we would say that it is of the utmost importance that the Lord's people be thoroughly rooted and grounded in this great doctrine of the plenary inspiration of Holy Scripture, and that having examined the evidence they be convinced that the Bible is the very Word of God. Since all of the other Christian doctrines are derived from the Bible and rest upon it for their authority, this doctrine is, as it were, the mother and guardian of all the others. We believe that the foregoing statements are facts which will stand the test of scholarship and of historical investigation, and that they will not be denied by any informed and honest-minded person.

While in our day the Bible has been sadly neglected even in many of the churches, we believe that the time is coming when the Bible shall have its rightful and honored place in the Church and in the affairs of men. At any rate we look forward confident that when the tumult is over, when the present storm of unbelief has subsided, the sacred heights of Sinai and Calvary will again stand forth, and that amid the wreck of thrones, extinct nations, and shattered moral principles, mankind, tried by so many sorrows, purified by so much suffering, and wise with so much unprecedented experience, will again bow before an omnipotent and merciful God as He is revealed in an infallible Bible.

www.ingramcontent.com/pod-product-compliance
Lightning Source LLC
Chambersburg PA
CBHW030132100526
44591CB00009B/615